60s
Fashion

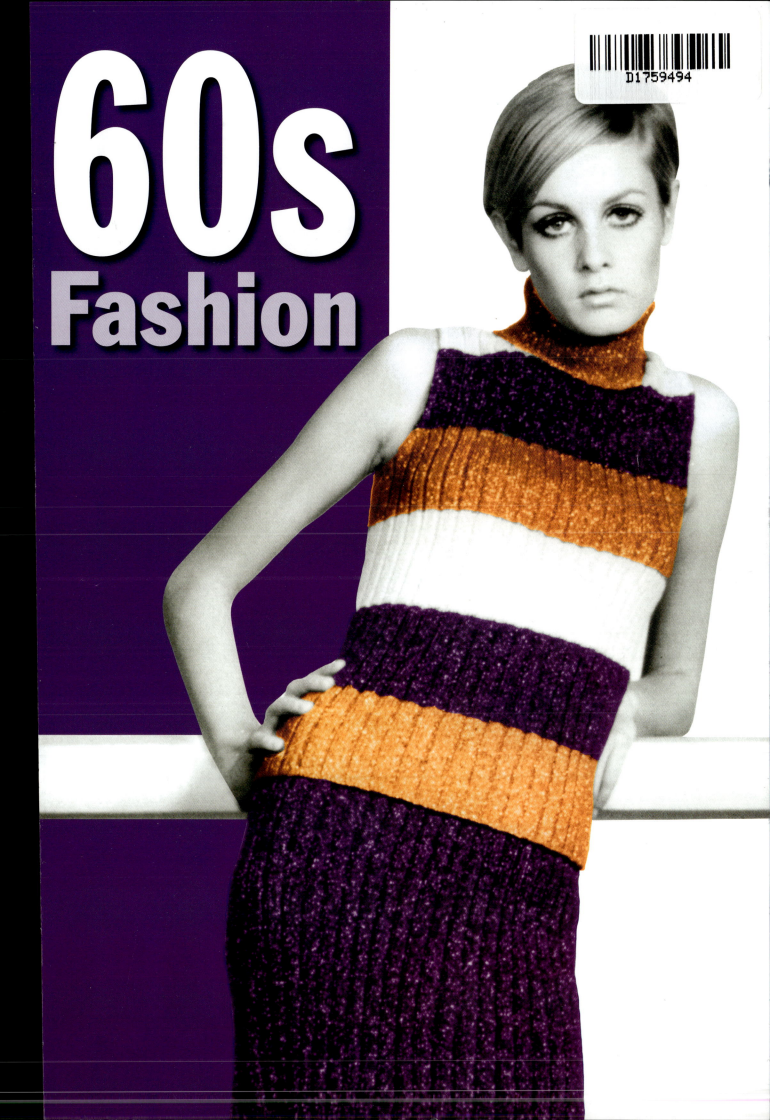

Contents

2

60s FASHION

3

First published in the UK in 2013

© Instinctive Product Development 2013

This edition published by Park Lane Books

www.parklanebooks.com

Printed in China

ISBN: 978-1-906969-33-2

Designed by: Tak Ho

Creative Director: Kevin Gardner

Written by: Michael Heatley, Nigel Cross, Mike Gent, and Helen Akitt

Images courtesy of PA Photos and Wiki Commons

Chapter One:
Introduction

The effects of the fashion breakthroughs and innovations of the Sixties are still to be seen on our streets and television screens. Conventions and drab colors were thrown aside as designers let their imagination run riot. Union Jack flags were daringly made into jackets, while miniskirts and other risqué outfits revealed the female form as never seen before… Even the space race left its mark, not only in futuristic styling but the use of plastic and other materials.

The Beatles may have made Liverpool the place to be as they started the Sixties music revolution but, as far as fashion went, Swinging London was undoubtedly "where it's at." The capital's youth had more disposable income than ever before and, with war, rationing, and National Service now ugly memories, they were ready, willing, and able to embrace the freedoms denied their parents.

The Sixties was the decade when fashion first grabbed the headlines with bold colors and aggressive styling, taking haute couture to the world and creating the vibrant looks we take for granted today. This publication celebrates the men and women that made the revolution possible, from designers through models to the photographers who shot them.

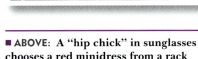

■ **ABOVE:** A "hip chick" in sunglasses chooses a red minidress from a rack of colorful outfits in London.
■ **RIGHT:** Bright colorful creations by Mary Quant.
■ **BELOW:** A typical scene on the King's Road, London, in the Sixties.

Chapter Two:
The Mod Generation

Mod was a peculiarly British movement. It originated in early-Sixties London without spreading significantly to America or Europe, although it did pave the way for the Swinging London scene that fascinated the world. Despite its parochial nature, the influences that created the distinctive Mod look came from a variety of different places.

The term "Mod" was derived from "modernist," a word used to describe young Londoners who were devotees of modern jazz.

At first, Mod was limited to a relatively small number of people who attended all-night jazz sessions at clubs like the Flamingo and the Americana. To reflect the stylish music, early Mods dressed smartly, in a manner that owed a debt to Ivy League fashions like box jackets and button-down shirts. This also served to distance them from fellow jazz fans notorious for their scruffy, beatnik attire.

Both venues were attended by American G.I.s stationed near London. These servicemen had

plentiful supplies of clothes that were hard to find in England and coveted by Mods – mainly Levi's jeans and Harrington jackets (named after a character in television soap opera *Peyton Place*) – which they were happy to sell. In addition, there was a strong European influence via Italian and French movies. For a certain time, everything French was cool; the Mods adopted the scooter as their favored mode of transport after seeing Gallic actor Alain Delon riding one in a movie.

■ OPPOSITE: Mods in their trademark uniform, riding scooters.

■ RIGHT: Mods were influenced by the French after seeing French actor Alain Delon riding a scooter in a movie.

■ BELOW: French actress Jean Seberg influenced early female Mods.

Gradually, by mixing and matching, the essential elements of the Mod look coalesced. Early Mods scoured London for the right clothes, and this obsessive quest constituted a large part of the movement's appeal. Hair was important too, but most barbers of the time simply cut men's hair rather than styling it, forcing the Mods to find hairdressers familiar with the Italian razor cut. Like much of Sixties fashion, the subculture was a reaction to the gray, post-war austerity of the Fifties. Mods were affluent, working in well-paid jobs, and able to indulge their passion for fashion.

At this point in the early Sixties, Mod remained an elitist movement and almost entirely male-dominated. Early female Mods sought the approval of their men by imitating the look of French movie stars like Jean Seberg. Later, the girls remained largely in the shadow of their boyfriends, adopting similar clothes and hairstyles, and this resulted in a somewhat androgynous appearance.

The Mod philosophy was all about attention to detail. Made-to-measure suits were a necessity, and individuals were fastidious about their preferences, such as the length of the side vents on their jackets, which ranged from 1" to 5", and the number of buttons – two, three, or four. Pants were always narrow, 14"-17", before bell-bottoms came in.

Shirts with pointed collars became as common as button-downs. Ties were also narrow, preferably knitted. Made-to-measure footwear was not uncommon, preferably imitation crocodile shoes or Cuban-heel boots. For a more casual look, they favored the "Fred Perry" – a three-button polo shirt marketed by the British tennis champion of the Thirties; this was often worn with a suit.

As the movement started to spread across London, the music of choice changed. The reverence for black American music remained but the focus shifted from jazz to the blues and R&B. By 1962, London had developed a thriving R&B scene, with bands like Blues Incorporated and the Rolling Stones at the forefront, but Mods preferred to dance to the original singles in clubs that specialized in playing recorded music.

1962 was the year in which Mod went overground when a *Town* magazine feature centered on a number of leading "faces," including Marc Feld, later Marc Bolan of T. Rex fame. For many of the original Mods, this marked the start of the movement's decline as it grew from an exclusive cult to a full-scale phenomenon.

Mod began to spread across the UK, especially to northern cities like Manchester, Liverpool, and Sheffield. Like Bolan, two other would-be stars who finally made it big in the Seventies, David Bowie and Rod Stewart, were Mods. Both were photographed sporting variations of a longer, late-period Mod hairstyle, with a short center half-parting and the hair brushed severely to either side.

Although the pioneering Mods sneered at the Rolling Stones and The Beatles, later converts were more inclined to listen to rock and

■ **OPPOSITE:** Mods were immaculately turned out; shoes were a particular feature.

■ **ABOVE:** A youthful Bowie was a Mod. His variation of a Mod hairstyle, with short center half-parting with the hair brushed to either side, is shown in this photograph taken in 1965.

pop bands. With Mod representing a sizeable demographic, it was inevitable that the music industry would target the subculture. Peter Meaden, manager of The Who and himself a Mod, was the first to attempt this. Although the members of The Who were not Mods, they were quickly given a makeover.

The band soon parted company with Meaden, but new managers Chris Stamp and Kit Lambert developed the image, introducing a pop-art element to their wardrobe with symbols like the Royal Air Force roundel (target) design and the Union Jack appearing on their clothes. Early singles, like *My Generation* and *Anyway, Anyhow, Anywhere*, referenced the Mod lifestyle, but The Who were savvy enough to discreetly disassociate themselves from the movement before it became passé.

The Small Faces were more like the genuine article, needing no image tweak to establish their Mod credentials – lead singer Steve Marriott's soulful voice and center-parted hairstyle among them. Like

The Who, they soon evolved beyond the confines of the movement. Selling bands to an audience that remained inherently suspicious of rock music proved tricky, as fondly remembered but less successful bands like The Action, the Creation, and The Birds (featuring a young Ronnie Wood) proved.

To keep warm on their scooters as they toured London's nightspots, the Mods adopted the Parka, a coat that had originated in the army, hence its khaki coloring. Practicality was quickly enhanced by fashion, as the fur-collared version with "fish-tail" rear pleat became the one to be seen in.

Scooters became synonymous with Mods for several reasons. Firstly, the two rival manufacturers, Vespa and Lambretta, were both Italian. The bikes were small and light and the encased engine

meant that no protective clothing was necessary for the rider (or pillion passenger) to keep clean. They were easily affordable on weekly installment-plan payments. Engine capacity ranged from 150cc to 200cc; at the time, in Britain, learners were permitted to ride vehicles of up to 250cc. Even more importantly for the hair-conscious Mod, crash helmets were not compulsory. Scooters gave Mods mobility and freedom from reliance on public transport, which stopped running long before they were ready to leave the clubs.

A fashion for customizing scooters quickly took hold. A fly screen affixed above the handlebars became the place to stick plastic letters spelling out the rider's name and hometown. Chrome racks, crash bars, and leopardskin seat covers were also desirable

■ **OPPOSITE ABOVE:** 1966 saw the emergence in England of a band calling themselves the Small Faces. They were formed in 1965 but in 1966 they released their first album, imaginatively titled *The Small Faces*. They identified closely with the Mod movement.

■ **OPPOSITE:** Two Mods sit on their scooters wearing fur-collared Parka coats. The bikes are covered with spotlights – a Mod fashion statement.

■ **ABOVE:** A pair of teenage Mod girls admire a finely customized scooter in the 1960s.

accessories. By 1964, handlebar mirrors were merely part of a large array of lights and mirrors festooning the front of the bike.

The extravagantly decorated Vespas and Lambrettas also served to heighten the tensions between the Mods and another British youth subculture of the era, the motorbike-loving, leather-clad Rockers. Mods saw Rockers as greasy, scruffy, and hairy throwbacks to the Fifties, while the Rockers held the Mods in contempt as effete and effeminate and mocked their scooters.

The conflict, fueled by the press, came to a head over two holiday weekends in 1964. Firstly, there was a widely reported confrontation in Clacton, a seaside town near London, over Easter. Then, in late May, further riots took place in two other south-coast resorts, Brighton and Margate. The beachside battles wrote themselves into English folklore and were widely reported in America. The music press and some musicians leapt to the defense

of the young people. Everyone took a stance – you were either a Mod or a Rocker.

With Mods demonized in the tabloid press as hooligans, it was clear that the movement was in decline. Other factors were at play, too; the dress code, which had once stood for individuality, had hardened into a uniform. Like other youth cults before and after, Mod became the victim of its own success, ubiquity robbing it of what made it special. The movement had even made it on to national TV. The Friday night music show *Ready, Steady, Go!*, first broadcast in 1963, was heavily Mod-influenced, complete with the hedonistic slogan "the weekend starts here." By 1964, the Mods even had their own monthly magazine. Whereas Mods were once obliged to search London for their clothes, the rise of Carnaby Street, the King's Road in Chelsea, and the Portobello Road in Notting Hill, now catered for the fashion-conscious male.

Mod style did eventually make some inroads into America. In the summer of 1965, designer John Stephen opened a boutique within a department store, Dayton's, in Minneapolis. *Look* magazine ran a feature entitled *The Minneapolis Mods*, predicting that the British look would take over the American fashion scene. This was not quite the case, but Stephen went on to open 20 more franchises across the States and Canada where it was previously believed that the average US male was too conservative for British clothes, despite the early Ivy League influence on Mod.

By 1966, Mod had started to fragment. The originals were growing up and leaving their youthful lifestyle behind them. Swinging London fashions had evolved directly out of the Mods' narcissistic obsession with clothes. Toward the end of the decade, skinheads took some elements of Mod fashion but added a harder, more brutal edge. In turn they would

■ **BELOW:** Mods and Rockers are seen racing along during a clash on Hastings beach in 1964 – the battles wrote themselves into folklore and were widely reported in America.

■ **ABOVE:** John Stephen opened more than 20 franchises of his store all over the United States and Canada.

■ **RIGHT:** Designer John Stephen.

mutate into the only marginally less threatening suedeheads, named for their slightly longer hair. In the mid-Seventies, the English northern soul scene displayed certain parallels with Mod as devotees danced enthusiastically all night to obscure American soul records.

1979 saw a full-blown if short-lived Mod revival in the UK. This was inspired partly by the success of new-wave rockers the Jam, whose leader Paul Weller was deeply committed to the Mod ideal. The other factor was the movie version of The Who's 1973 album, *Quadrophenia*, featuring Sting in an early acting role. The movie recreated the Mod lifestyle of 1964, including the climactic beach fights. The same year of 1979 saw the emergence of 2-Tone, a multi-racial movement directly linked to Mod; the same genre finally became big in America in the mid-Nineties. Even the Brit-pop bands of the same era demonstrated more than a little Mod in their DNA.

With enclaves now in such unlikely places as China and Mexico, it seems that Mod has finally transcended its very British origins.

Chapter Three:
Pop Idols

By the early Sixties the rebellious spirit of rock'n'roll had largely been tamed. A new breed of pop idol had emerged, manufactured by record companies to appeal to teenage girls. Previously, the rock'n'roll image of leather jacket and jeans had been popularized by movie stars James Dean and Marlon Brando, as well as musicians. Squeaky-clean teen icons like Paul Anka, Bobby Vee, and Bobby Darin wore traditional suits on stage, sometimes adopting a more relaxed Ivy League look for record sleeves and publicity shots.

Sixties pop-star fashion did not establish an identity of its own until the arrival of The Beatles. It's a well-known part of Beatle lore that manager Brian Epstein insisted the band ditch their leather stage wear in favor of suits and ties in order to make them acceptable to the show business establishment. The success-hungry Beatles were happy to go along with the change, although John Lennon would later express his contempt for it.

The early Beatle stage suits were subtly different, and, along with the mop top hairstyles, established an original, distinctive look while remaining within existing traditions. Their collarless suits were the work of London tailor Douglas Millings and resembled a similar design by Pierre Cardin. The suits were made of wool mixed with mohair and were usually pale gray in color. The long lapels concealed just three buttons. In keeping with the trend of the times, the pants were narrow and pressed to a razor-sharp crease. Between 1963 and 1967, Millings, with his son Gordon, was

responsible for The Beatles' stage outfits and some of the clothes they wore off duty.

Just as The Beatles' music developed, so their working clothes went through various changes. Millings' original design remains the most recognizable and iconic, although a new model had actually superseded it by the time of their first US visit in 1964. The revised design had a shorter jacket and velvet collar and was most famously

seen in the movie *A Hard Day's Night*, as well as on that American tour. The record-breaking appearance on the *Ed Sullivan Show* saw the Fab Four sport a special dark gray version.

Just about anything The Beatles were seen wearing quickly became a fashion item. John Lennon's 1964 Greek fisherman's cap and the black polo-neck sweaters worn by the band on the cover of *Rubber Soul* in 1965, were just two examples.

- **OPPOSITE:** The Fab Four pose in "Beatle" suits. (Ronald Grant Archive/ Mary Evans)

- **ABOVE:** The Beatles perform on the *Ed Sullivan Show* in 1964; they are wearing their next phase of suits.

- **LEFT:** "Beatle" boots, previously worn by George Harrison, on show ahead of sale at an auction. These ankle-length boots were actually called Chelsea boots, but were popularized by Beatles fans.

Ankle-length Chelsea boots with a Cuban heel and elasticized sides quickly became known as Beatle boots and were the footwear of choice to complement the suit.

Beatle fashion was quickly picked up on by their fans, and retailers on both sides of the Atlantic soon exploited the trend. Huge amounts

of merchandise became available, particularly in the States. London's rag trade offered made-to-measure Beatle suits, but purchasers were often surprised to discover the difference in quality between stage clothes, designed to be worn a handful of times, and everyday wear.

The vogue for military-style jackets that took hold in Swinging London can also be traced back to The Beatles. For their appearance at Shea Stadium in 1965, the Fab Four wore tan collarless jackets based on army styles, with epaulettes, button-down breast pockets, five buttons, and a large

■ **LEFT:** Trendy young men outside Dandie Fashions (Tailoring For Men), one of the shops for the "Dedicated Follower of Fashion" in Swinging London, King's Road, Chelsea.

■ **BELOW:** The Beatles' psychedelic shop in Baker Street, pictured behind scaffolding.

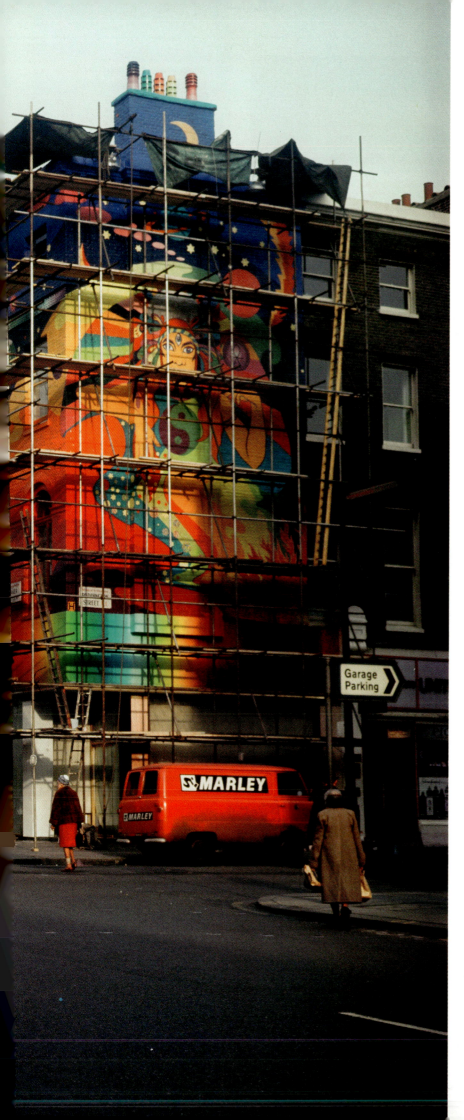

60s FASHION

rear pleat. The jacket was also seen in the movie *Help!*.

The vogue for real military jackets began when the boutique, I Was Lord Kitchener's Valet, started selling surplus supplies in 1966. Eric Clapton was the first pop star to indulge, but it was Mick Jagger who started a craze when he bought a Grenadier guardsman drummer's tunic and wore it on television. The Fab Four responded with the brightly-colored military uniforms seen on the cover of *Sgt. Pepper's Lonely Hearts Club Band*.

When The Beatles set up their Apple organization in late 1967, fashion retailing was one of their first new ventures. The Apple Boutique in London's Baker Street was notorious for the psychedelic mural that upset the city authorities. The shop closed after only eight months, The Beatles giving the remaining stock away but only after keeping the best items for themselves. Meanwhile, the former Dandie Fashions on the King's Road, Chelsea, had been transformed into Apple Tailoring, but the made-to-measure clothing outlet was equally short-lived.

The Rolling Stones sported matching houndstooth jackets for their first British television appearance. But, as they developed their image as the bad-boy antithesis of The Beatles, their appearance changed accordingly. Hitherto members of bands had tended to display uniformity in their look. The Stones went against this, establishing their own individual dress codes and remaining defiantly uncategorizable, mixing beatnik attire with items of clothing associated with both Mods and Rockers.

Whatever they wore, the Stones were labeled scruffy by the British press, with much derogatory comment about their "long and unkempt hair." The band and

■ **LEFT:** Brian Jones of the Rolling Stones with a rather eclectic outfit.

■ **BELOW:** A Terylene advert featuring Dave Davies from The Kinks, 1966.

■ **OPPOSITE:** The Jimi Hendrix Experience: Noel Redding, Jimi Hendrix, and Mitch Mitchell.

KINK THINK: THIS 'TERYLENE' IS SMOOTH

'Smooth,' said Dave of the Kinks, when he saw Ina in her 'Terylene' suit. 'Still smooth,' they both said a dozen pictures later—after lots of sitting, kneeling, curling-up action. But then 'Terylene' has never crushed, never needed ironing after washing.

Suit by Carol Freeman in 58/-. 'Terylene' 45/- wool, worsted. Style 'Belinda'. About 14½ gns.

manager Andrew Loog Oldham willfully played up to this image. In reality, original guitarist Brian Jones was something of a peacock who loved to dress in the finery of the period and to be seen in the fashionable nightspots of Swinging London.

The Kinks were another new band to discover that a little controversy never did any harm. In staid post-war Britain, their name caused a few raised eyebrows, but that was nothing compared with the outrage that greeted the dark pink hunting jackets the band wore in early appearances. Songwriter and singer Ray Davies was a quiet, private man who satirized the prevalent male narcissism in the band's 1966 single, *Dedicated Follower Of Fashion*. His brother, lead guitarist Dave, was the dandy of the outfit and, like Brian Jones, was often seen in the coolest clubs. Dave was sufficiently famous to become the face of an advertising campaign for clothing made from the synthetic fabric, Terylene.

By 1967, London had established a reputation as a fashion Mecca. On arrival, visiting American musicians, particularly those from the San Francisco scene, would immediately make their way to Carnaby Street or the King's Road to check out the latest gear.

Jimi Hendrix relocated to England in order to kick-start his career under the management of former Animals bassist Chas Chandler. Jimi's fashion sense was as startling as his innovative guitar technique and was just as much his own creation. Initially, Chandler kitted out Hendrix and his band, the Experience, in conventional two-piece stage suits, which Jimi hated.

For an important London showcase gig in January 1967, at the Saville Theater, owned by Beatles manager Brian Epstein, Hendrix defied Chandler and clothed himself and the band in the British capital's most colorful threads. The three men also sported matching curly perms. Hendrix, a former US paratrooper, loved military-style apparel, particularly the famous British Royal Hussar jacket he was once ordered to remove by an outraged London policeman. He also favored psychedelically patterned shirts and jackets, extravagantly decorated flared pants,

and a range of accessories that included scarves, rings, medallions, and, on occasion, a feather boa.

The Beach Boys were originally known as the Pendletones, a name suggested by Mike Love in homage to the plaid woolen shirts made by the Pendleton company of Portland, Oregon. The band's early look helped further popularize the shirts throughout the United States. The cover of their 1963 album, *Surfer Girl*, shows The Beach Boys holding a surfboard and wearing matching blue Pendleton shirts.

Fellow Los Angeles outfit The Byrds represented the epitome of Californian cool. Before John Lennon began wearing his granny-style glasses (also known as Ben

Franklins) in the movie *How I Won The War*, in 1967, Byrds lead singer Roger McGuinn made small rectangular sunglasses his trademark. McGuinn bought his own after seeing a girl fan with a pair at a gig at LA venue Ciro's, starting a trend for undersized sunglasses of various shapes. By the end of 1965, *Time* magazine was moved to comment on the style, referring to them as "hoot-owl glasses." Band member David Crosby was not to be outdone in the fashion stakes. His jazz-influenced green suede cape caused a minor sensation, particularly on the band's first visit to England where The Byrds were briefly touted as America's answer to The Beatles.

The pop industry in the Sixties was very much male-dominated. Originally a member of folk group The Springfields, Dusty Springfield went solo late in 1963 and turned to pop. Her fashion sense was as distinctive as her soulful singing voice. The combination of pencil skirt, thick black eyeliner, long eyelashes, and bouffant hairstyle was relatively easy to replicate and spawned a thousand imitators. Dusty was one of the most successful British female singers of the Sixties and enjoyed six Top 20 hits on the *Billboard* Hot 100.

Stateside success eluded one of Dusty's main rivals, Sandie Shaw, who was famous in the UK for appearing on television singing in bare feet. Her "natural" image included designing her own clothes. After success in the *Eurovision Song Contest* in 1967, Sandie's singing career began to tail off and the following year she married Welsh designer Jeff Banks and launched her own fashion line, selling clothes and, ironically, shoes.

Marianne Faithfull is inextricably associated with the Rolling Stones. Having been discovered at a party by their manager, Andrew Loog Oldham, her very public relationship with Mick Jagger sometimes overshadowed her singing and acting careers. Marianne's clothes were made for her by designer Caroline Charles, who dressed many other stars, including Jagger. Charles' brand of apparel was popular in America

■ ABOVE LEFT: **Dusty Springfield had a very distinctive style with bouffant hair, thick eyeliner and, often, pencil skirts.**

■ ABOVE: **Marianne Faithfull wears a coat by Daniel Hechter, 1967.**

■ OPPOSITE: **George Harrison with his long hair and beard.**

too. Although she claimed not to be overly influenced by fads, Marianne's preferences – gloves, boots, and miniskirts – made her the archetypal Sixties girl. Perhaps her most famous item of clothing, though, was the fur rug in which she was draped at the time of the drugs raid on Redlands, Keith Richards' country house, in 1967.

As The Who had shown when they became Mods, bands often looked to the street for sartorial inspiration. Late in 1969, English rockers Slade, managed by Chas Chandler, became the first group to adopt a skinhead look. But this worked against them because of the movement's association with violence and was dropped as soon as their hair grew again.

The Beatles remained trailblazers until the end of the decade, by which time their multi-colored finery had been replaced by utilitarian denim, and hair, previously carefully coiffed, now grew longer and flowed freely. This, along with the obligatory beards, made John Lennon and George Harrison in particular almost unrecognizable from their earlier mop top incarnations. The journey of the Sixties' leading pop idols and fashion icons was complete.

Chapter Four:
From Quant to Cardin: The Designers

The concept of clothes designers hitting the headlines caught fire in the Sixties. Who you wore was as important as what you wore, and the fashion halls resounded to some superstar names.

Biba

Founded by Barbara Hulanicki (born 1936), Biba was the first shop to sell high-fashion clothes aimed at teenagers at an affordable price point. Its first success came in May 1964 when a pink gingham dress, offered by mail order to readers of the *Daily Mirror* newspaper, sold some 17,000 units. Brigitte Bardot had recently worn a similar dress. The first Biba store, in Abingdon Road in Kensington, opened that September.

Biba's Swinging London look was represented by long tight sleeves, short hemlines, and high shoulders. Colors were drawn from a palette of brown, sepia, gray, and plum. Cathy McGowan, presenter of popular TV music show *Ready, Steady, Go!*, was a Biba style icon.

A second store opened in 1965 in Kensington Church Street and a series of mail-order catalogues followed in 1968. Biba closed in 1977, but the brand has undergone sporadic relaunches. Hulanicki now designs capsule collections for UK high-street company, Top Shop.

André Courrèges

André Courrèges, born in France in 1923, was a latecomer to fashion, having studied engineering. His so-called Space Age collection of 1964 featured outfits with cutout midriffs and backs that were worn without a bra. These were matched with flat boots, goggles, and helmets, their shape and style inspired by the equipment worn by astronauts. The look was geometric and used bright colors, while his use of materials such as plastic pushed the fashion envelope.

Courrèges also brought us the miniskirt (though Mary Quant would dispute that honor), the pantsuit, the go-go boot, and established the triangle-shaped shift dress as the defining silhouette for female Sixties fashion. His designs were widely copied by others and sold at lower price points; after his 1964 breakthrough, the market was flooded with plastic skirts and jackets, angular seaming, crash helmets, white boots, and goggles. Other innovations included hip-hugger pants teamed with halter-tops, transparent tops, and sequined jumpsuits.

Givenchy

The names of Hubert de Givenchy (born in 1927) and the Sixties' most elegant actress, Audrey Hepburn, are inseparable. Givenchy's designs were used in Hepburn movies, such as *Charade, Paris When It Sizzles, How To Steal a Million, and Breakfast At Tiffany's*, for which he designed the most famous "Little Black Dress" of all time. She wore his designs off screen, too.

Other famous patrons of his fashion house, established in 1952, included Empress Farah Pahlavi and Marella Agnelli, as well as the Guinness, Grimaldi, and Kennedy families, who wore Givenchy to the funeral of John F. Kennedy.

Givenchy's fashion house has since featured on the résumés of such names as John Galliano, Alexander McQueen, and Julien MacDonald.

■ **OPPOSITE:** The Biba boutique in London, 1966.

■ **ABOVE:** Sixties fashion models wear Courrèges' designs at Harrods, 1968.

■ **BELOW:** Audrey Hepburn wearing that "Little Black Dress," designed by Givenchy, in the movie *Breakfast At Tiffany's*.

Mary Quant

Mary Quant, born in London in 1934, is said to have been the inventor of the miniskirt and, later in the decade, hot pants.

She opened Bazaar, a boutique on the King's Road, in 1955, at a time "when fashion wasn't designed for young people," and was influenced by Chelsea beatniks and dance outfits remembered from childhood. Her clothes combined simple shapes with strong colors. In the early Sixties, her designs were bought by the chain store JC Penney to be mass-produced for the American market. In 1963, a second branch of Bazaar opened in Knightsbridge, while she later launched a lower-priced line, the Ginger Group, to appeal to a wider clientele.

She gave the miniskirt the name of her favorite make of car, explaining that: "It was the girls on the King's Road who invented the mini. I was making easy, youthful, simple clothes, in which you could move, in which you could run and jump and we would make them the length the customer wanted. I wore them very short and the customers would say, 'Shorter, shorter.'"

Mary Quant, who was awarded the OBE in 1966, later moved into cosmetics.

Oleg Cassini

Like Givenchy, French-born American fashion designer Oleg Cassini (born in 1913) was best known for one client – the First Lady, Jacqueline Kennedy. Having served in the US Cavalry alongside Ronald Reagan in wartime, he opened his own fashion business in New York, building on pre-war experience designing for Hollywood movie studios.

Ossie Clark

A latecomer to the scene, Raymond "Ossie" Clark, born in Liverpool in 1942, was nevertheless a name synonymous with cutting-edge fashion in the late Sixties and beyond.

Having won a scholarship to the Royal College of Art, he graduated in 1965 with a first-class degree – the only one awarded that year – and three months later his graduation collection appeared in British *Vogue*. Simultaneously, Clark began designing for Alice Pollock's shop, Quorum. The pair married, and worked together until 1973. He pioneered the midi as well as the maxiskirt, while his pants for women became fashion essentials.

Clark delighted in new shapes, silhouettes, and textures. He fearlessly mixed different prints in the same garment, used a range of surface decoration – embroidery, appliqué, beads, and lacing – and also worked with unusual materials, such as snakeskin.

The self-proclaimed "Secretary of Style" to the White House also dressed actress-turned-princess Grace Kelly, to whom he was briefly engaged, helping create her timelessly elegant look. His influence on bridal wear still resonates today – the "Jackie look" he created being called "the single biggest fashion influence in history" by Hollywood designer Edith Head.

■ **OPPOSITE: Model Dian Poore with a selection of Mary Quant bags at the leather goods, luggage, and handbag fair.**

■ **ABOVE LEFT: Jacqueline Kennedy with couturier Oleg Cassini (as Indian), at the Plaza Hotel, New York.**

■ **ABOVE: A 1960s outfit designed by Ossie Clark; it is worn by model Suki Poitier.**

Paco Rabanne

Though his name is nowadays most associated with perfume, Paco Rabanne, born in 1934, brought Spanish flair to French fashion. He left his native country for France when the Civil War broke out and even made it to Hollywood, designing costumes for Jane Fonda's hit movie *Barbarella*. Singer/actress Françoise Hardy was also a big fan of his designs.

Originally a jewelry designer, Rabanne started his fashion career designing jewelry for other houses before trying his hand at clothing. He soon became known for his eclectic fashions, and his clothing was equally as decorative as his early creations. He started his own fashion house in 1966, and combined materials such as metal and paper with garish vibrant colors in his outlandish and flamboyant designs. Rabanne reveled in his reputation as the *enfant terrible* of the Sixties French fashion world.

■ **LEFT:** Minidresses by Paco Rabanne, in London in front of a London Bus, late 1960s.

■ **OPPOSITE ABOVE:** Pierre Cardin takes off into space with his girl of the future, but presents some more contemporary designs here with dashing young navy flashed with white, matching legs, 1967.

■ **OPPOSITE:** Yves Saint Laurent brought the masculine pantsuit to the 1967 fashion picture in a series of faultlessly tailored models. Shown here, is one in navy and white pinstripe wool with bell-bottom pants, vest, and white shirt. The feminine touch came in the platform black patent leather sandals. A white panama hat and polka-dotted tie and handkerchief tucked into the breast pocket completed the ensemble.

Pierre Cardin

Pierre Cardin, born in 1922, was a designer who combined the flair of his Italian birthplace with his French education to make his own indelible fashion mark. He founded his house in 1950. In 1959, he was expelled from the Chambre Syndicale for launching a ready-to-wear collection for the Printemps department store, but was soon reinstated.

Cardin favored avant-garde looks, such as thigh-high boots, colorful shift dresses emblazoned with bold symbols, and collarless jackets. He loved geometric shapes, while he brought displaying the designer's logo on the garments into haute couture for the first time. His clothing was often unisex.

Yves Saint Laurent

Born in 1936, Yves Saint Laurent grew up in Algeria. Moving to Paris, he found a job assisting Christian Dior and took over his fashion house in 1955. He opened his own in 1962, and was soon dazzling the critics with his ingenuity and wit. His 1965 Mondrian-inspired shift dresses and 1966 gangster-style pantsuit, known as *Le Smoking*, were innovations; others were safari jackets for men and women, tight pants, and thigh-high boots.

Saint Laurent had women wear tuxedos and fedoras, reimagined working-class garments like the pea coat and the peasant blouse in luxurious fabrics, and created a new fashion template with a subversive streak.

He was also the first French couturier to come out with a full ready-to-wear line, opening his Rive Gauche prêt-à-porter boutique in 1966; future designer Miuccia Prada, then a student, was a customer.

Chapter Five:
Cool London

■ LEFT: Carnaby Street was the hottest of the world's fashion hotspots, pictured here in 1967.

■ ABOVE: John Stephen's clothes, modeled here on a catwalk, found a ready market with Mods.

■ OPPOSITE: Lord John shop in Carnaby Street, London, in the 1960s.

Swinging London was born in April 1966 when *Time* magazine proclaimed London the world city of the decade. The term "Swinging London" was used several times in the cover story. London had been out of the cultural spotlight as Beatlemania diverted attention to the provinces, but its sudden blooming saw John, Paul, George, and Ringo trade their Liverpool homes for pads in the Home Counties. Thanks to *Time*, Swinging London was firmly in the forefront of the world's imagination and would remain there for years to come.

Youth and money were the twin factors that turned London from a gloomy, grimy post-war capital into a bright, shining epicenter of

style. Its population was younger than it had been since Roman times, thanks to the post-war baby boom – in fact 40% of the mid-Sixties population was 25 or younger. National Service for men had been abolished in 1960, and a combination of more freedom and fewer responsibilities made Sixties youngsters unrecognizable from their parents' generation. Little wonder they rebelled against any and every limitation and restriction of post-war society.

Rationing was now a distant memory, and Londoners had more disposable income than ever before to spend. Weekly earnings in the UK in the Sixties outstripped the cost of living by 183% – an amazing figure

bettered in London, where earnings were higher than the national average. The prime beneficiaries were music and fashion.

For a while, Carnaby Street was the hottest of the world's fashion-related hotspots. Situated between Oxford Street and Regent Street, in the heart of London's West End, this relatively small thoroughfare was a magnet for bohemian types and a center for tailors and dressmakers, and it offered rents that were relatively cheap for the area. It was tailor-made for the new age. As stuffy convention was brushed aside, to make way for color, imagination, and daring, Carnaby Street was where it was at.

Trendsetters, rock stars, Mods,

artists, hustlers, models, tourists, designers, all thronged to Carnaby Street to play their part in creating one of London's most vibrant scenes. By the end of the decade, Carnaby Street rivaled Buckingham Palace as one of London's most popular attractions.

The Carnaby Street story had begun in the previous decade when John Stephen opened His Clothes in 1958. Stephen, a Glaswegian who had come to the capital in 1952 at the age of 19, saw an opportunity in offering good quality but fresh designs to a young crowd who had a little more money to spend than their parents at the same age. Influenced by the smart yet casual look of Italian fashion, Stephen provided flamboyance in place of boring convention, and individual style instead of humdrum clothing for the masses.

Stephen's clothes found a ready market with Mods. Soon they were thronging the street, snapping up the latest looks, not just from Stephen's growing empire that included Male West One but also a host of other boutiques including Mates, Kleptomania, and I Was Lord Kitchener's Valet. The imaginative names were a sure sign of changing attitudes, pairing imagination with wit and a large dose of fun.

Lord John was another notable addition to the growing Carnaby Street fashion parade. Opened by the three Gold brothers in 1963, it tapped into the Mod ethic, selling up-to-the-minute styles that kept pace with their rapidly changing tastes. Often confused with the rival John Stephen empire, Lord John attracted a famous clientele of bands and musicians including the Small Faces, The Who, and Brian Jones of

the Rolling Stones. Micky Dolenz of the Monkees paid a special visit to Britain in 1967 to buy six suits from the shop.

Time magazine had pictured the street on its front cover in 1966, stating that "Perhaps nothing illustrates the new swinging London better than narrow, three-block-long Carnaby Street, which is crammed with a cluster of the 'gear' boutiques where the girls and boys buy each other clothing."

The coverage that followed in the mainstream media inevitably chipped away at Carnaby Street's cool image. The Kinks poked some gentle fun at the kind of people who packed the road in their 1966 song *Dedicated Follower Of Fashion*, with the line "Everywhere the Carnabetian Army marches on, each one a Dedicated Follower of Fashion." A place that had seemed so anti-establishment just a few years before was now subject to the same kind of mockery as the conventional world.

Further west, the King's Road in Chelsea and Portobello Road were other fashion hotspots. Women were lured there by Mary Quant's radical miniskirts, which flew off the rails of her iconic Bazaar store. Quant was the undisputed queen of the group known as the Chelsea Set, a hard-partying, eclectic mix of "toffs" and working-class movers and shakers.

Granny Takes a Trip was started by ex-history graduate Nigel Waymouth to sell girlfriend Sheila Cohen's collection of antique clothes. However, the arrival of John Pearse from Savile Row to create outrageous, experimental clothes for the well-heeled Chelsea set put the shop, and the area, on the map.

In the Portobello Road, the original I Was Lord Kitchener's Valet also specialized in antique

■ **ABOVE:** Mary Quant, British Mod fashion designer, 1967.

■ **OPPOSITE ABOVE:** A military jacket as worn by John Lennon in the 1960s.

■ **RIGHT:** *Ready Steady Go!* hostess Cathy McGowan interviews Ringo Starr, 1964.

"Carnaby Street is my creation. I feel about it the same way Michelangelo felt about the beautiful statues he created."

– **John Stephen**

clothing. It peddled a line in Victorian and Edwardian military jackets that quickly became popular with rock royalty – the cover of *Sgt. Pepper* depicted the Fab Four in military jackets, and guitar legend Jimi Hendrix sported one on the front of his debut LP, *Are You Experienced?*, which he bought from the shop.

The London club scene was where pop's peacocks hung out to show off their amazing dress sense. The mid-Sixties magnets for this elite social set were clubs like the Ad-Lib and the Bag O'Nails where, in the words of one commentator, "the sons and daughters of the aristocracy could rub shoulders with the new working-class aristocrats – pop stars." Later in the decade, the focus shifted to the UFO Club in the bohemian Soho district and, later still, the Roundhouse in Camden.

Several movies attempted to capture the Swinging London of the period, but the most potent promoter of London style and fashion went out weekly on the ITV television network. Hosted by Cathy McGowan, *Ready, Steady, Go!* told the nation's youth what they were supposed to be wearing the following week; in that respect, it was the British counterpart of *American Bandstand*. The look, the style, and the music came in one neatly wrapped, off-the-peg packet ready to buy.

By 1967, the media in general had tired of Carnaby Street stories. As with popular music, the focus was moving elsewhere, and America's West Coast, specifically San Francisco, would – for a while, at least – be "where it's at."

But every time you see a miniskirt or watch a band steal a look from the past with military or Union Jack jacket, the spirit of Swinging London, and Carnaby Street, lives on.

Chapter Six:
Twiggy, Shrimp, Bardot, and co.: the Supermodels

■ **BELOW LEFT:** Peggy Moffitt, pictured in 1965.

■ **OPPOSITE:** The front cover of *Harper's Bazaar* for July 1967, featuring a beautiful Jean Shrimpton wearing makeup from Barbara Gould, Chanel No. 22 perfume, hair by Michael at Leonard, and earrings by Adrien Mann.

■ **OPPOSITE BELOW:** Twiggy, modeling the shrunken woolen look, 1966.

The clothes of the Sixties were groundbreaking – but they would not have made the impact they did without the women who wore them.

This was the era that created the supermodel. And London was, as ever, the epicenter of the revolution. Models are still waif-like today, and when current clotheshorse Kate Moss said, "Nothing tastes as good as skinny feels" she acknowledged this. Moss has also advertised cosmetics with the less controversial slogan "Get the London look" – proof that the capital's name and reputation live on.

Peggy Moffitt

Born in Los Angeles in 1940, Peggy Moffitt started as an aspiring actress, appearing uncredited in the 1955 movie, *You're Never Too Young*. As a model, she developed a signature style; her heavy eye makeup was described as Kabuki-like, drawing on Japanese theater. Her signature hairstyle was the five point cut, a hair-do created by Vidal Sassoon and named by the five angles to the style.

A photograph of Moffitt wearing a topless monokini bathing suit, designed by Rudi Gernreich, made headlines in 1964. She retained the rights to his designs after his death, and arranged for them to be displayed in an exhibition titled *The Total Look* at the Los Angeles Museum of Contemporary Art's Pacific Design Center. This celebrated her work with not only the designer but also her photographer husband, William Claxton.

JULY 1967 3/6

HARPER'S BAZAAR

LIVING
WITH
BEAUTY

OUR
BEAUTY
EDITOR'S
OWN
SLIMMING
STORY

BEAUTIFUL
CLOTHES
BEAUTIFUL
HOMES
BEAUTIFUL
PEOPLE

BAZAAR
BEAUTY BOX

Jean Shrimpton

The world's first acknowledged supermodel, "The Shrimp" was born in Buckinghamshire in 1942, the daughter of a wealthy English builder. Her modeling career began in 1960 when photographer David Bailey discovered her. They were briefly engaged, and their relationship was dramatized in a TV movie, *We'll Take Manhattan*, in 2012. She appeared on the cover of *Harper's Bazaar* and *Vanity Fair*, but more unusually also graced US non-fashion periodicals *Time* and *Newsweek*.

The tall (5' 9½") Shrimpton set the style for so many of the Sixties supermodels, appeared on 20 *Vogue* covers, earned an unprecedented $120 an hour, and helped raise hemlines around the world when she attended a 1965 race meeting in Melbourne, Australia, in a shift dress with a hemline four inches above the knee. Her sister Chrissie was well known as Rolling Stone Mick Jagger's girlfriend.

Troubled with "enormous guilt for earning so much money" for doing "tough and immensely tedious" work, Shrimpton happily slipped from view after being eclipsed by Twiggy. She now runs a hotel in Cornwall, where she has lived as a virtual recluse with her husband since quitting the fashion industry.

Twiggy

Born Lesley Hornsby, in 1949, Twiggy became as emblematic of the Swinging London of the Sixties as the Beatles, Stones, and Kinks. Originally nicknamed "Sticks" because of her reed-thin figure, she switched it to "Twigs" and, finally, "Twiggy." A model for a scant four years, she had never even walked the runways by the time she exploded onto the scene in early 1966.

Her figure was androgynous, her eyes heavily made up, and her haircut fashionably short. The "Twiggy" was extremely short and cut to a point at the back of the neck, parted in the middle, gelled down, and worn tucked behind the ears. She visited the United States for the first time at the age of 18, and inspired a Twiggy Barbie as well as lunchboxes, false eyelashes, pantyhose, sweaters, tote bags, and paper dolls.

Twiggy proved she was not just a pretty face by developing a career as a singer in the Seventies. She acted in plays by George Bernard Shaw and Noël Coward, enjoyed a spell as a TV host, and wrote several books, including an autobiography, 1998's *Twiggy In Black And White*.

Twiggy is still very much around in the current millennium, most notably as a regular model for UK high-street chain Marks & Spencer.

Veruschka

Real name Vera Grafin Von Lehndorff-Steinort, this German-born model (born in 1939), traded under her Christian name long before Madonna was invented. She was the first superstar model of the Sixties, and her six-foot-plus frame, with its improbably long limbs, was mold-breaking, following as it did the more womanly shapes of the models that came before her.

She appeared on 11 *Vogue* covers and in one classic movie – *Blow Up*, Michelangelo Antonioni's innovative movie about an arrogant, handsome fashion photographer (David Bailey, most viewers assumed) on the prowl in Swinging London. Veruschka's five-minute part was that of a top fashion model, photographed by actor David Hemmings.

Life magazine called her "The Girl Everybody Stares At," while the fashions she wore were usually exotic haute couture inventions from designers like Scaasi rather than Mary Quant's more streetwise creations. She intentionally let her life be clouded in mystery, so that queries into her past often raised more questions than they answered.

She returned to the catwalk at age 71, content in having changed fashion for good. "In the Sixties," she said, "fashion was about liberation. It was about setting women free."

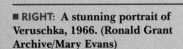

■ **RIGHT: A stunning portrait of Veruschka, 1966. (Ronald Grant Archive/Mary Evans)**

■ **OPPOSITE: Pattie Boyd, wearing beret style headwear, 1964.**

Pattie Boyd

Pattie Boyd, born in 1944, got her break when working as a beautician. She was asked to model by a client who turned out to be an agent. She was a shy, innocent girl-next-door type, whose trademark was dark eye makeup and pale lips; as well as modeling, she wrote a monthly column, "Pattie's Letter from London," for *16* magazine.

She inspired Twiggy to start modeling in 1966, by which time a TV commercial promoting Smith's crisps had led to her appearing as an actress in The Beatles movie *A Hard Day's Night*. During the shooting (she played a Mary Quant-clad schoolgirl) she would meet future husband George Harrison.

They married in 1966 but she left him in 1973 for Eric Clapton. She was the inspiration for his writing *Layla* when she was the unattainable wife of his friend, while Harrison for his part wrote *Something* for her. (Clapton's *Wonderful Tonight* was also written for her.) To complete the picture, her sister Jenny married Mick Fleetwood of Fleetwood Mac.

Boyd, now a photographer, and resolutely single, published her autobiography in 2007, saying, "Given my life over again, I wouldn't change anything."

Celia Hammond

Another of David Bailey's muses, Celia Hammond (born c. 1943) did most of her work between 1963 and 1968 and was frequently featured on the cover of *Vogue*. She formed a close working relationship with photographer Terence Donovan, while unrelated singer/songwriter Donovan wrote *Celia Of The Seals* as a tribute to her attitude.

Hammond became a vegetarian in her teens, and while at first happy to model fur, she later became concerned about the cruelty of the fur trade and took a stand against fur. She saw television footage of the Canadian seal cull and told of her horror in a press interview. Contacted by Lady Dowding of the charity Beauty Without Cruelty,

Celia agreed to fly to the Gulf of St. Lawrence as an observer of the seal cull for BWC. Having witnessed the appalling cruelty, she immediately vowed never to model fur again and persuaded all the top models of the day to give up promoting fur.

Celia had a long relationship with guitarist Jeff Beck. She now devotes her time to rescuing animals.

■ ABOVE: Celia Hammond, modeling the Simone Mirman Spring and Summer Collection, 1962.

Brigitte Bardot

Although she was only briefly a fashion model, was not a part of the Swinging London scene, and first made her name in the Fifties, Brigitte Bardot was still very much a face and figure of the Sixties.

Born in Paris in 1934, she made the cover of *Elle* magazine at 16. Two years later she moved into movies, encouraged by photographer and future husband Roger Vadim. "I started out as a lousy actress, and I have remained one," she's said. She attracted great interest in the United States, but never seriously pursued her career there.

Vadim directed her in *And God Created Woman* (1956), the movie that turned "BB" into a global sensation. Two years later she retreated to the south of France but spent the Sixties in and out of the public eye.

Bardot officially retired from acting in 1973 when she was 39. Since then she has devoted herself to animal rights activism.

■ **ABOVE & RIGHT: The star of** *And God Created Woman*, **Brigitte Bardot.** (Ronald Grant Archive/Mary Evans)

37

Penelope Tree

"Only Vogue could make a Tree," said *Playboy* magazine in its review of 1968, the year that Penelope Tree made her breakthrough. The daughter of Marietta Tree (a United Nations representative) and Sir Ronald, a former Member of Parliament, and friend of Winston Churchill, she had been discovered in 1966 by *Vogue*'s editor Diana Vreeland when she appeared at the Black and White Ball, thrown by writer Truman Capote at the Plaza Hotel, in an outfit with slits that revealed her briefs and pantyhose.

For a while she rivaled Jean Shrimpton and Twiggy as London's favorite fashion face and figure. According to famed photographer David Bailey: "Penelope Tree is the most original model there's ever been. She's the most original-looking girl I've ever seen." She quit modeling in the early Seventies, a combination of a nervous breakdown and a skin complaint explaining her sudden disappearance, and married Beach Boys pop star Ricky Fataar.

■ **ABOVE:** Makeup artist Paul Richards of Eylure demonstrated his panda look on model Penelope Tree, November 1969.

Wilhelmina Cooper

A Dutch model born Wilhelmina Behmenburg in 1939, she moved to the States at age 15 and became a successful model. She holds the record for most covers on American *Vogue*, appearing 27 times. During her cover-girl days, Wilhelmina boasted that she was "one of the few high-fashion models built like a woman" and had a classical, aristocratic look that became popular.

In 1965, she married Bruce Cooper, former executive producer of *The Tonight Show Starring Johnny Carson*. They founded Wilhelmina Models, which rivaled the all-powerful Ford Models as the era's leading model agency.

Cooper died of lung cancer in 1980. Her obituary in *Time* magazine ran: "With her 5' 11", 38-24-36 frame, doe eyes, delicate cheekbones, and mane of high-piled dark hair, she epitomized the classical, aristocratic look that she helped to make the style standard of the Fifties and Sixties..."

FORTUNE

$2.00/December 3, 1979

The Embattled Presidency:
What the Candidates Say

Better Prospects for
Productivity

WILHELMINA OF
WILHELMINA MODELS INC.

UGLY COMPETITION
FOR PRETTY FACES

■ **ABOVE:** The last photoshoot of Wilhelmina Cooper.

Chapter Seven:
Capturing the Look: Famous Photographers

While the new breed of supermodels may have been the faces that brought the new styles on to the high street in the new decade, it was the men who photographed them that were just as important. Fashion photography came of age in the Sixties.

The decade saw a new wave of photographers whose skills and originality were often matched by their larger-than-life personalities, and many of them entered the public consciousness in much the same way as rock singers, movie stars, and models. They quickly became as famous as the people they photographed.

Sir Cecil Walter Hardy Beaton, CBE was granddaddy of them all – the *eminence grise* to the new generation of young guns. Beaton was a celebrated fashion, portrait, and war photographer, painter, and award-winning costume designer, who'd picked up the basics of the camera from his nanny who had a Kodak 3A folding model. In the Thirties, Beaton made his mark with *Vogue* and *Vanity Fair* magazines and, later, as a photographer of the Royal Family and wartime leader Winston Churchill.

Even in the Sixties he was still at the top of his game, and his influence was far-reaching, via

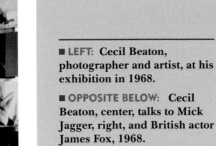

■ LEFT: Cecil Beaton, photographer and artist, at his exhibition in 1968.

■ OPPOSITE BELOW: Cecil Beaton, center, talks to Mick Jagger, right, and British actor James Fox, 1968.

■ BELOW: Beaton also listed painting among his accomplishments. Here, he poses with his portrait of Mick Jagger, 1966.

his shots of such icons as model Twiggy, singers Mick Jagger and Barbara Streisand, and actors like Albert Finney and Audrey Hepburn, not to mention American First Lady Jackie Kennedy.

It was under his tutelage that **David Bailey (CBE)**, a young working-class lad from the East End of London, made his first forays into this brave new world. The two met when they were working at British *Vogue* and Bailey was very influenced by Beaton's stark use of square format (6" x 6") images.

Bailey and fellow East Ender, **Terence Donovan**, were at the forefront of the fashion revolution in the UK. They began to transform the art of photography by anticipating other movements and styles before anyone else did. After completing their National Service, both of them worked for John French's studio, then described by Brigid Keenan, fashion editor of the *Sunday Times*, as "a finishing school for photographers."

Donovan came to prominence via his work for *Man About Town* magazine, and his East End background brought a tough, street vibe to his work. His shots of "spy scenes," which were done before the Bond movies, gave his model, Peter Anthony, the opportunity to screen test for the role of Agent 007.

Bailey set up his own studio in 1960 and swiftly rose to fame with his fabled "Autumn Girl" shot. On a fall fashion shoot for the *Daily Express* newspaper, he asked the model to kneel on the ground in a circle of leaves and peer at a squirrel. "That's what started it all," he'd later say. Donovan told him, "This picture's a breakthrough," and fashion guru Mary Quant would later observe that no fashion picture had ever been taken like that before. "It was a great slap of excitement; it was tremendous."

Bailey photographed real people in real situations. In the early Sixties, he transformed the Young Idea section of *Vogue* and, in one year alone, shot 800 pages of editorial for the magazine. For many of his shoots he used model Jean Shrimpton, who'd later comment about their meteoric rise: "I think our success was mainly down to timing. Everyone had been very elegant and I was a mongrel by comparison and he was as well – he portrayed me as a natural, rather scruffy girl."

By the end of 1964, Bailey had secured his place at the high table of Swinging London with his highly commercial release, *Box of Pin-Ups*, a box of poster prints

whose subjects included actor Terence Stamp, The Beatles, Mick Jagger, Cecil Beaton, dancer Rudolf Nureyev, artist Andy Warhol, and East End gangsters the Kray Twins.

His personal life ensured that the good-looking young snapper was soon as famous as his many subjects. Though married to Rosemary Bramble, he publicly dated Shrimpton, and later went on to marry French screen goddess Catherine Deneuve and, later still, British model, Marie Helvin.

Sir Norman Parkinson, CBE, the celebrated English portrait and fashion photographer who had turned fashion photography upside-down in the Forties,

called Bailey, Donovan, and Brian Duffy, another young Londoner instrumental in defining the spirit of the Swinging Sixties, "the Black Trinity." They broke the mold of fashion photography. The staid old guard felt threatened by these freewheeling young men in leather jackets, who took their models on to the streets and snapped them with small newfangled 35mm cameras.

Their inventive compositions were looser than the stiff, stuffier studio portraits of the Fifties. Duffy later observed: "Before 1960, a fashion photographer was tall, thin, and camp. But we three are different: short, fat, and heterosexual. We were great mates but also great competitors. We were fairly chippy and if you wanted it you could have it. We would not be told what to do."

If Bailey and Co were the *enfants terrible* of the new era, others also made their own distinctive contribution. In direct contrast to their working-class backgrounds, **Patrick** (later Lord) **Lichfield** was the son of Viscount Anson and Princess Anne of Denmark, and was the Queen's first cousin once removed. However, he transcended his upbringing to become a photographer of world renown and enjoyed a 40-year career, which later included the formidable task of shooting the official photographs at the wedding of the Prince of Wales and Lady Diana Spencer.

He made his break into photography in 1962, after leaving the Grenadier Guards. Starting out as a photographer's assistant on £3 a week, he made the most of his show business and aristocratic connections. Working from his studio in Pimlico, he soon had a little black book full of potential models, including Joanna Lumley, Jill Kennington, and Jacqueline Bisset. A flamboyant

■ **OPPOSITE ABOVE:** David Bailey, at home in his bedroom, c. 1960.

■ **OPPOSITE:** The front cover of *Queen* magazine – a stylish handbook of the Swinging Sixties for the fashionable and hip, featuring Jean Shrimpton, archetypal 1960s model, photographed by David Bailey and wearing a fine-spun Liberty print dress by Susan Small.

■ **ABOVE:** An early portrait of Norman Parkinson in his studio.

dresser, Lichfield quickly rose to prominence with his trusty Olympus in hand and snapped everybody, from Mick and Bianca Jagger on their wedding day, to the Duke and Duchess of Windsor in exile. Lichfield's memory of the latter encounter was of deliberately falling off his chair to force smiles out of his straight-faced subjects. The result got him a contract with *Vogue* magazine. He also worked for a range of other newspapers and magazines, including *Life*.

One of his most iconic images in the Sixties was the naked pose of singer Marsha Hunt, complete with a huge Afro hairdo, for the musical *Hair*. Another, was *Swinging London*, which featured Roman Polanski, David Hockney, and Lady Antonia Fraser. Other famous subjects included actors Michael Caine and Susannah York, comedian Peter Cook, playwright Joe Orton, and a host of Sixties glitterati.

In some respects, Lichfield took the lead set by his distant relation by marriage, **Lord Snowdon**, who had started his career 10 years earlier in exactly the same way from a studio in Pimlico under his real name of Antony Armstrong-Jones. Famous for his 18-year marriage to Princess Margaret, Jones was another talent whose playboy lifestyle almost succeeded in overshadowing his talents as a photographer.

He became the artistic adviser of the *Sunday Times* magazine, and established himself as one of Britain's most respected photographers. Though starting out in fashion, he went on to document images of inner-city life and the mentally ill, yet remains known for his portraits of public figures published in *Vogue and Vanity Fair*.

It may have seemed as if the world revolved around Cool Britannia in the Sixties but there were other equally influential

■ LEFT: Patrick Lichfield quickly rose to prominence in the Sixties.

■ ABOVE: Lord Snowdon, pictured with Princess Margaret at their wedding in 1960, was a hugely talented photographer.

photographers at work who helped to define the look of the era.

In the United States, **Richard Avedon** transformed photography in the Fifties and his influence exerted a big influence into the next decade. His stark imagery and brilliant insight into his subjects' characters made him one of the premier American portrait photographers. His extensive work for the likes of *Harper's Bazaar*, *Vogue*, and *Look* gave him access to celebrities from a wide range of disciplines. Famous for his unique style – minimalistic but well lit and often shot against a white backdrop, Avedon lensed the likes of Mae West, Pablo Picasso, and Robert Oppenheimer. And when he returned to guest-edit *Vogue* in April 1965, the cover shot of Jean Shrimpton, wearing a space-suit-inspired pink helmet, was taken by Avedon himself.

One of Avedon's most important protégés was Yasuhiro Wakabayashi, later known as **Hiro**. Born to Japanese parents, Hiro grew up in Shanghai, but in the mid-Fifties came to the US, where he was mentored by both Avedon and by Alexey Brodovitch, art director at *Harper's Bazaar*.

Working at first primarily with hand and foot models, he elevated images of shoes and watches, nail polish, and jewelry, to the level of art – typically focusing on an arresting contrast (setting off a dainty pedicure against a bed of octopus tentacles and rocks, or coiling a diamond tennis bracelet so it looked like a strange, creeping sea anemone).

Though not as well known as some of his *Vogue* colleagues, and his work for the magazine not as

■ **OPPOSITE:** Richard Avedon was one of the premier American portrait photographers.

■ **ABOVE:** A visitor looks at photographs of Hollywood actress Marilyn Monroe in the exhibition the "last sitting" at the museum of movies in Potsdam, Germany. The pictures, by American photographer Bert Stern, were taken in June 1962, two weeks before Monroe died.

vast, Hiro was nonetheless highly influential and, in 1969, won the prestigious Photographer of the Year award given by the American Society of Magazine Photographers.

Bert Stern similarly was at the top of his game in the Sixties and hugely successful in the worlds of fashion and advertising photography, working for *Vogue*, *Glamour*, and *Life*, as well as companies like Revlon and Smirnoff. One of his biggest claims to fame was the spellbinding 1962 "last sitting" photo session he did with Marilyn Monroe.

Other notable fashion photographers from the USA included Polish-born **Melvin Sokolsky**, famed for his "Girl in the Bubble" series of photos shot in Paris in 1963, and **Bob Richardson**, who brought a gritty sexuality to the fashion world. Though born in New York, **William Klein** relocated to France where he became known as much for his movie making and painting as his photography, but he contributed some bizarrely original fashion to *Vogue* and other magazines.

In France, **Jeanloup Sieff** was top dog, shooting mainly in black and white and famous for his big angle lensed style while, in Germany, **F. C. Gundlach** was the most significant fashion photographer, who shot a record 180 covers for fashionable young women's magazine *Brigitte* and was influenced by the Op-Art and Pop-Art Movements.

Without these visionary, skilled figures the Sixties fashion revolution would simply never have happened in the way it did and had such a huge impact on daily life.

Chapter Eight:
Deeply Hippie

The "peace and love" movement started out as a San Franciscan music revolution in 1965 but quickly became something bigger. A new counterculture slowly fanned out across the US and on to Britain and Europe.

At first, "hippies" – Sixties counterparts of the Fifties Beat Generation – were a small minority, but they soon found their own voice. The term hippie derived from the word *hip* and the synonym *hep*, which first surfaced in slang around the beginning of the 20th century and was probably based on the Forties term *hipster*: "a person who is keenly aware of the new and stylish."

Unlike Mod, hippie was never just about fashion. It had some deep-rooted philosophies and a political agenda – many were out to change the world in the late Sixties as the Vietnam War raged, while workers and students clashed with the authorities on the streets of Paris and London.

■ **ABOVE:** The "flower power" look involved very bright colors and eclectic patterns.

■ **RIGHT:** Hippies gather for a peace festival, 1967.

■ **OPPOSITE ABOVE:** A floral print kaftan became popularized by the flower power generation, worn usually with bare feet!

Its influence extended not just into music but literature, art, movies, environment, and lifestyle. Psychedelic drugs were also central to the hippie lifestyle, and "longhairs" experimented widely with LSD and marijuana, which were considered benign. This contrasted sharply with the pill-popping Mods, whose wide use of Purple Hearts meant that they were always on the lookout for a tussle with rivals the Rockers. The effects of these mind-altering substances manifested themselves in painting and music and in new clubs and ballrooms, such as the UFO in London, the Fillmore in San Francisco, and the Paradiso in Amsterdam – and, not surprisingly, in clothing too.

As 1966 turned into 1967, heralding the Summer of Love, the Regency Dandy/Carnaby Street Fop look was giving way to less formal styles. If the Fifties had been gray and the early part of the Sixties

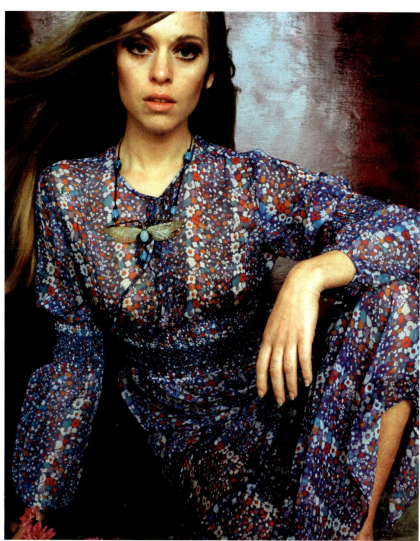

black and white, then the hippie movement turned the last years of the decade positively Dayglo!

As hippie took hold, a new series of boutiques catered to the new clientele in London: Granny Takes a Trip in Chelsea, Kleptomania in Chelsea and in Kingly Street (just round the corner from Carnaby Street), and I Was Lord Kitchener's Valet in Ladbroke Grove, Britain's answer to San Francisco's Haight-Ashbury, the birthplace of hippie culture.

Hippie fashions changed quickly. Flower power, as its name suggested, brought with it floral designs, especially the use of daisies, as well as swirling psychedelic patterns and swirls, and, though it was short-lived, its influence was long lasting. One minute it was all paisley styles, the next kaftans. As Kleptomania's proprietor Tommy

Roberts observed: "Out went red guardsman's tunics, Union Jack kipper ties, Victorian-style lacy minidresses, soul music, and anything to do with Swinging London. In came trumpet-sleeved kaftans, gypsy fringed shawls, psychedelic posters, joss sticks, peace and love badges, Frank Zappa, and Jefferson Airplane."

From early on, the hippie movement showed an obsession with all things Eastern. Ditching Western materialism and traveling to the East in search of spiritual enlightenment caught on in a big way, especially when the Hippie Trail opened up – a cheap way of getting from London to India and Nepal, via Istanbul, Tehran, Kabul, Peshawar, and Lahore. Loose flowing robes, kaftans, Afghan jackets and waistcoats, and Nehru jackets were quickly absorbed into the new look.

The Nehru jacket, a single-breasted tight-fitting, hip-length coat with its stand-up collar based on the garment worn by India's Prime Minister Pandit Jawaharlal Nehru, became hugely popular when The Beatles and acolytes like Donovan studied transcendental meditation with the Maharishi Mahesh Yogi in the summer of 1967.

Women went bra-less, and the highly popular miniskirt was given a rival in floor-length maxiskirts. Empire-waisted sequined numbers that sported exotic, funky sleeves, and halter-neck dresses with bare backs, also came into vogue. Floral granny dresses were another highly popular item, and the sight of young girls walking along Sunset Strip in Los Angeles in these dresses, styled after Twenties and Thirties female fashions, inspired fabled Californian rockers, Moby Grape, to write the song *Hey Grandma*.

The so-called Age of Aquarius saw wide use of fabrics like velvet and crushed velvet, silks, and satins. Accessories were an integral part of hippie garb, especially for girls – love beads, headbands, nose rings, ankle bracelets, sandals, granny glasses with tinted lenses, and earrings. There was also wide use of buckskin and fringed suede and leather, based on the American Indian and Wild West styles of the 19th century. Bell-bottom jeans and pants continued to be in fashion for both sexes with the new generation. Headwear such as floppy felt hats and leather cowboy hats were also soon part of hippie attire while, for men, beards and mustaches became popular; both sexes let their locks grow out.

One of the big innovations in the later Sixties was the advent of big outdoor festivals and free concerts.

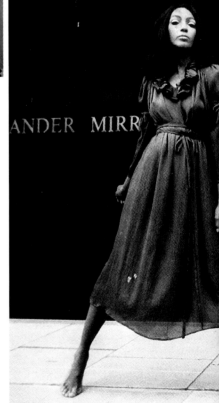

Hippies believed in communing with nature and body painting, so bare feet and nudity came into fashion at these tribal gatherings – hence the much-used phrase "let it all hang out." The front cover of British rock band Free's second album famously featured a shot of a nude young woman taken at the 1969 Isle of Wight Pop Festival, while the musical *Hair* climaxed with the actors disrobing and inviting members of the audience to divest and join them.

By mid-1969, the penchant for eye-catching psychedelic clothing had subsided. As one critic observed, the crowds heading toward the stage area of Eric Clapton's Blind Faith free concert in London's Hyde Park in June '69, wore "not the florid kaftans and beads of a couple of years back but a reversion to the denim/gypsy/beat, generally drab apparel that preceded the flower era."

The half-million people who congregated a month or so later at the Woodstock Festival in New York State reflected this even more – men were draped in the Stars and Stripes flags or sober army surplus jackets their contemporaries were wearing in Vietnam. There was still a splash of color at this gathering, thanks to singer Janis Joplin, who wore gold and beaded bangles,

■ **OPPOSITE: Indian religious spiritual leader Maharishi Mahesh Yogi, 1968.**
■ **BELOW: A hippie fashion show, 1968.**
■ **RIGHT: A hippie lady, with large hat and eye makeup, at the free Rolling Stones concert in Hyde Park, London, 1969.**

feathers, and a wide-sleeved tunic of chiffon and velveteen.

The audience at Woodstock displayed a growing fondness for one of the more popular styles associated with the hippie movement, that of the tie-dying of shirts, vests, jeans, and T-shirts – accomplished by folding the material into a pattern, binding it with string or rubber bands, and applying dye to only parts of the material. The ties prevent the entire material from being dyed and create a pattern that is different every time. British singer Joe Cocker was famously photographed on stage

at the event sporting a tie-dyed granddad vest.

What will be remembered about the hippie era is that it was a time when anything worked for fashion. As with most movements, however, many of its innovations were quickly absorbed into the mainstream, and, though elements such as long hair, frayed jeans, bell-bottom pants (renamed flares), and full-length skirts and dresses would be carried over into the super-excessive Seventies, the early part of the next decade would not be able to hold a candle to the colorful fashion highs of the late Sixties.

Chapter Nine:
Hair

As with clothes, hairstyles started the new decade continuing the conformity of the Fifties. As the Sixties wore on, hair displayed more diversity and change than could ever have been predicted, reflecting the enormous social and cultural shifts the new decade wrought in society.

Women's hairstyles

As the Fifties turned into the Sixties, the **bouffant** – big, smooth, backcombed, and set with lacquer – remained hugely popular and was favored by figures as different as Jackie Kennedy, a style-setter throughout the decade, and early in their careers by pop stars like Dusty Springfield and The Supremes.

1960 saw the arrival of the voluminous **beehive**, created by Margaret Vinci Heldt of Elmhurst, Illinois, who had been asked by *Modern Beauty Salon* magazine to come up with a style that would reflect the coming decade.

■ **TOP:** Audrey Hepburn was one of many who adopted the beehive hairstyle, which originated in 1960.

■ **ABOVE:** The "Twiggy" hairstyle was named after the supermodel who popularized the cut.

■ **LEFT:** A smooth, sleek bob by quintessential Sixties hairdresser, Vidal Sassoon.

■ **OPPOSITE:** Marsha Hunt, star of the musical *Hair*, wearing a silk coat and satin pants, helped popularize the "Afro," 1969.

As its name suggests, the style was a distinctively hive-shaped, backcombed mountain of hair set in place like the bouffant with clouds of lacquer.

Adopted by movie stars like Audrey Hepburn, it caught on like wildfire and was soon popular with the masses. Beehives could also be twinned with longer hair worn half up, half down, as modeled by the likes of Brigitte Bardot and the Ronettes. Both styles were also often worn with headscarves and the very fashion-conscious might also wear a pair of dark sunglasses – a look popularized by the First Lady.

As with clothing, the Mod movement exerted a huge influence on hairstyles with their often blunt and angular look. The easy-to-wear and flexible **bob** had been around in one form or another since the start of the century – the hair is cut straight around the head at jaw level and often worn with a fringe. It gained a new lease of life when Mod girls started to wear it short with a heavy, straight-cut fringe and was soon taken over by figures like fashion designer Mary Quant.

The short Mod bob was defined by Quant and **Vidal Sassoon**, who revolutionized women's hairdressing and became the byword in hair chic. He was the first hairdresser superstar, creating iconic styles and popularizing short hair with asymmetrical and geometric cuts. Sassoon became firm friends with Quant and she'd famously say to him, "I made the clothes, but you put the top on."

Other styles popular with young women in the mid-Sixties included the "**Twiggy**," named after the supermodel who pioneered the androgynous look, mentioned before. The **five point cut**, worn by Peggy Moffitt, was another created by Sassoon.

The **bowl cut**, meanwhile, was favored by both men and women. Mods liked to wear it to jaw level, but rock stars like Brian Jones of the Rolling Stones, with whom the style became synonymous, adopted a longer version.

Driven by social change, political activism, and psychedelic rock music, hair became longer in the late Sixties for both sexes, and was left to grow more naturally in keeping with the hippie philosophy, which preached a more organic and free-and-easy approach to life.

Many young hippie women wore their hair long and straight, frequently "un-styled" compared to a few years earlier. It was often worn center-parted with or without a fringe. Long hair was also often put up into a ponytail or adorned with feathers, leather bands, and flowers. Girls in more mainstream society tended to favor the chin-length contour and the **pageboy** look.

Young black people in both the US and UK favored the "**Afro**." Previously it had been socially acceptable for black women to straighten their hair, but with the advent of the Civil Rights Movement, many started to leave their locks to grow out naturally as a symbol of racial pride. By the close of the decade the Afro was a popular style, created by combing the hair away from the scalp and allowing it to extend from the head like a halo. It was popularized by singers like Marsha Hunt and political activists like Angela Davis, but men, including guitarist Jimi Hendrix and singer/keyboard-player Billy Preston, favored the style; white underground icons, like UK singer Julie Driscoll, also adopted it.

Men's hairstyles

The Fifties had seen a transformation in the way men wore their hair. A staggering proliferation of hair-styling products, particularly setting sprays, hair oil, and hair treatments such as Brylcreem pomade, helped create such iconic styles as the pompadour, Duck's Ass, flat top, and bouffant. The new decade would go on to produce even more variety and diversity. The Sixties began with close-cropped and clean-cut styles but by its end conformity had given way to complete anarchy.

The **crew cut** was a hugely popular carry-over from the Fifties, a look made iconic by such movie stars as Steve McQueen. It derived from the strict short back and sides of the military and involved trimming the sides until they were almost completely shaved and letting the top grow out a little longer.

If there was one style that defined the look of the Sixties trendsetter, it had to be the **mop top**. The mop top was a bowl-shaped haircut that had a fringe trimmed just above the eyebrows and often covered the ears. The description came from the similarity to a shaggy dish mop. The mop top made its first appearance in 1963 and was made popular by The Beatles, hence their nickname. The style was equally popular with many of the British Invasion bands that followed in their wake, such as Herman's Hermits, The Yardbirds, and The Dave Clark Five.

As each year of the Sixties went on, men's hair slowly crept further and further over the shirt collar. At first just a shaggier version of the mop top look, by the end of the decade, it was the longest it had been worn in the UK since the 18th century.

■ **OPPOSITE:** Steve McQueen with a crew cut hairstyle in 1960.

■ **ABOVE:** The Beatles influenced a generation with their "mop top" haircuts.

■ **RIGHT:** Peter Noone, of the pop group Herman's Hermits, wears a longer length "mop top."

Outside of fashion centers like London or San Francisco, having long hair could get you into serious trouble. It wasn't just the hurled insults of "Is it a girl or is it a boy?" Long hair led to wearers not being served in bars, getting into fights or, if you lived in the American South, even worse, as the characters in late-Sixties groundbreaking movie *Easy Rider* found to their cost.

It wasn't just the locks that grew. Facial hair was also back in vogue, and not just long sideburns or the trimmed goatee look of the beatnik era. Beards were now stragglier and longer. Mustaches, too, were hip. The Beatles had been sporting them since 1966, but after *Sgt. Pepper* they became fuller and more prominent. The handlebar style reeked of the old Wild West or World War I military, while rock stars like John Lennon and David Crosby famously sported the "walrus."

However, not all young men liked the longhaired look. Some went for the radical **skinhead** style

that was exactly what it said on the label – a shaved (but not bald) head. Skinheads hated the hippie look and philosophies, and the close-cropped head finished off a "uniform" that included short-sleeve, button-up shirts, Sta-Prest pants or Levi's jeans, Crombie-style overcoat, and Doc Martens footwear, popularly known as bovver boots.

Hair in the Sixties had been on a rollercoaster ride, from the elegant, smart, and groomed looks of the early Sixties enjoyed by the Mods, to the opposite extreme 10 years later – the carefree shoulder-length style of the hippies. These changes reflected the adaptation, experimentation, and invention for which the decade became famous.

■ OPPOSITE: **John Lennon with long hair and a beard.**

■ ABOVE: **Even James Bond (Sean Connery) sported a mustache in the late Sixties.**

■ LEFT: **Skinheads hated the hippie look and had a very alternative appearance, as shown here.**

Chapter Ten:
The Legacy of Sixties Fashion

The Sixties saw an explosion of color, change, and optimism in all things, as a reaction to the Depression of the Thirties, and the rationing that followed World War II in most of Europe. While we can see evidence of this in the home decor of the day, it was in fashion that this was most prominent.

We talk glibly of the "Swinging Sixties," but this is a vast over-simplification. There was no such thing as a single Sixties look. For the first time in history there was a multitude of co-existing, exciting looks, reflecting the fact that this was a turbulent and exciting time in society.

Like the political and social changes of the decade, clothing trends were groundbreaking and brought completely novel ideas to the landscape of fashion. While designers still defined trends for the season, for the first time ever counter-culture groups like London's Mods and America's hippies influenced styles and clothing types that were produced by mainstream fashion brands and marketed to young people. The Sixties was fashion and beauty by the young for the young.

For women, the Sixties defined new ways of looking glamorous, as typified by the heavy eyeliner and vamp hairstyles. But they did not just change women's fashion – it was a time when menswear became eclectic and important, as

■ **OPPOSITE:** Love Stockings from McCallum boutique, New York. Black crepe culotte dress, from Hilderbrand, March 1968.

■ **RIGHT:** A classic simple Sixties look, with white knee-high boots.

■ **BELOW:** Twiggy in a classic pose in the Sixties.

it remains today. Men began to use clothes to define their place within society – there were Mods and Rockers, paisley-clad beatniks, and polo-necked artists all using clothes to create their identity in a time of unprecedented change.

Moreover, the pace at which communication was improving meant that young people could keep up with new trends, and TV and magazine advertisements fed their desires.

By the end of the Sixties, most people had TV and, although most broadcasts were still in black and white at this time, magazines were full of color prints. Color fashion plates had started appearing in magazines such as *Vogue* in the late Thirties, but the Sixties also brought the trend for hip photographers such as David Bailey. They took fashion photos as never before and started an enduring trend for more life-like poses in fashion models.

The legacy of Sixties fashion is all around us – notably the iconic fashion plates of the day, hems and heels of all lengths, jeans and casual wear acceptable for both sexes in most everyday situations, and possibly most momentous of all – trousers and pantsuits as normal day and evening wear for women. What was unthinkable in 1960 is commonplace today, and it started in the Sixties.

Synthetic fibers

The Fifties had produced a war-backlash glamorous look for women – all full skirts and bright red lipstick – but this was a look for everyone and one that persisted for a number of years. They had also seen the emergence of a whole new range of synthetic fabrics – nylon, first commercialized in 1939, had grown to 20% of textile output by the end of the Fifties. The concept of "wash and wear" fabrics that emerged in the Fifties was consolidated during the Sixties with fabrics such as polyester and acrylic, and polyurethanes such as Spandex and Lycra. Fabrics became more durable and color more permanent. New dyeing effects were being achieved and shape-retaining knits offered new comfort and style.

In the early Sixties, synthetic fiber accounted for nearly 30% of American textile mill consumption. By 1965, the manufactured fiber industry was providing over 40% of the nation's fiber needs. The opportunities these provided for designers to produce fashionable, colorful and, above all, affordable, clothing for young people were immense.

Skinny models

For better or worse, one of the legacies of Sixties fashion is the ultra-thin model. Prior to the Sixties, the curvy French "Bardot" figure had prevailed – and in the Fifties it was not fashionable in Europe to appear too thin after the privations of rationing. The Sixties brought times of plenty, and thin models such as Jean Shrimpton and Twiggy appeared on the scene. Their beanpole bodies could best display the shift and straight Mary Quant minidresses of the era.

This obsession with thinness that started in the Sixties with models like Twiggy is one of the more controversial legacies. Arguably it has caused women, including those in the modeling and entertainment industries, to suffer from serious eating disorders and fatal illness.

■ **LEFT:** "Wash and wear" fabrics, shown here made of nylon and Terylene, were made popular in the late Fifties and into the Sixties.

Fashion weeks

The New York Fashion Week (1943) can claim to be the first, designed to attract attention away from French fashion during World War II, when fashion industry insiders were unable to travel to Paris to see French fashion shows. But renewed European interest in fashion in the Sixties and a resurgence of European designers saw the launch of London Fashion Week in 1961, and Paris Fashion Week was relaunched in 1973. Today most major capital cities around the world boast annual events rooted in the growing interest generated in the Sixties to show off the talents of their local designers.

■ **LEFT:** A knee-length culotte suit in navy corduroy by Christian Dior. The single-breasted jacket has small revers and long sleeves and the knee-length culottes are trim and slim fitting. The news vendor's cap is in matching corduroy. The bright, "surprising" orange sweater and hood have ribbed wool stockings to match. The outfit is modeled by Jean Shrimpton, 1965.

■ **BELOW:** Twenty-four of Britain's models spent nearly 1,000 hours rehearsing for London Fashion Week, 1962.

Enduring fashion trends

Trousers/Pantsuits

It is only necessary to look as far as the concept of pants and pantsuits for women in order to see how much of what we take for granted today was groundbreaking in the Sixties. It's hard to believe that not so long ago pantsuits were considered a fashion no-no in the work place, and that women were discriminated against because they chose to wear pants.

Introduced in the Sixties by designers such as Yves Saint Laurent, they started a revolution in the way women could dress comfortably, but at the same time caused a controversy that would rage for another 30 years. It was only in the Nineties that the US Senate finally allowed woman senators to wear pantsuits during sessions of Congress. Even today, some conservative institutions like banks, government agencies, and law firms may still disapprove of the pantsuit for women.

Trousers and the pantsuit now appear on the catwalks every year in new feminine styles that flatter the figure and embrace modern trends. Women who "live in jeans" have the liberating years of the Sixties to thank for this possibility.

Miniskirts

The mini was a small piece of fashion that was the biggest influence of its time. The miniskirt undoubtedly influenced the rise in hemline for all fashion – such as shorts, hot pants, schoolgirl skirts, baby-doll dresses, and cut-off denims.

The mini signaled that the length of the hem was no longer a restriction in female attire. Although it was the shortness of length that shocked at the time, its legacy was the liberation of hem length. Subsequent decades have seen hems rise and fall with increasing rapidity and, today, dresses and skirts can be bought in most lengths – from floor-length to pelmet (to be worn with leggings, of course).

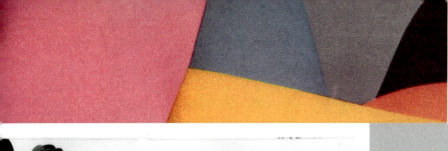

■ **OPPOSITE:** A model wears black woolen pants with a red and gold broche jacket and matching blouse created by Coco Chanel, 1964.

■ **LEFT:** Women wearing miniskirts and minidresses at the Indianapolis Motor Speedway, 1969.

■ **BELOW:** A variety of stockings and tights in brilliant opaque spring colors, from hosiery designers with names like Grosvenor Gaytones and Sunarama. The printed pink and gray Corfam shoe is by Kurt Geiger, 1967.

Pantyhose

Prior to the Sixties, the well-dressed woman was mostly wearing seamed stockings with suspenders, and hemlines had to be kept modestly low enough not to reveal these. The advent of the miniskirt meant that an alternative to stockings was required and pantyhose took over – within two years they had 70% market share. During the same period, hosiery manufacturers moved away from knitting flat and, instead, pantyhose were knitted in a tube, with the result that nylons with seams virtually disappeared.

The new expanse of leg available to designers plus the advances in technology also resulted in the Sixties trend for patterned pantyhose. Although the fashion for plain versus patterned varies from year to year, today, hosiery has never been available in so many styles. A wide range of new products is now available, ranging from body-toning control-top pantyhose and hold-ups to moisturizing and massaging pantyhose. The advent of pantyhose, coupled with the increasing acceptance of pants for women, also led to the development of leggings as a fashion item (rather than just sportswear).

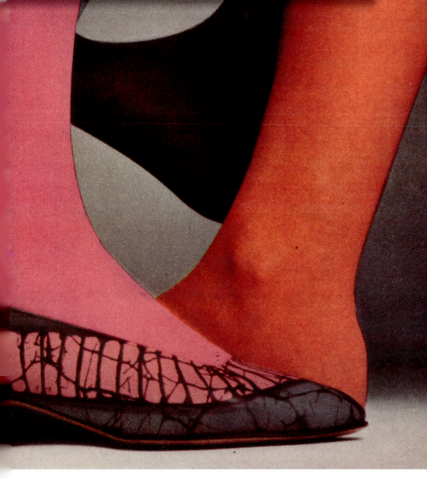

Bell Bottoms

Bell-bottom or wide-legged pants revivals have occurred numerous times across the history of fashion, but the Sixties were most influential in that they set the stage for the future of pants. For the first time, wide-legged pants were worn by men for everyday use – and, without the bell-bottom, the denim trend may not have become the default style choice of young men (and women) today.

By introducing a casual pair of trendy pants into the closet of every American youth, bell bottoms made "cool comfort," acceptable to wear every day. Pants as casual, comfortable wear, rather than being stiff and formal, are a direct descendant of Sixties fashion.

Other fashions that originated in the Sixties and still impact on fashion today include:

- Knee-high boots for everyday wear – the Sixties took a utilitarian work-wear item and adapted it into its own unique style, as seen with variations of riding boots and Western boots (cowgirl/cowboy boots).
- Heels of all heights and widths.
- The Sixties' high fashion and formal wear revival of the early 19th-century empire waist finds its way into fashion every season. A style that's commonly found in Seventies maxidresses is reinvented every summer by modern fashion in its casual summer collections, appropriate for casual weekends involving everything from a beach-vacation getaway to a flexible, feminine look while grocery-store shopping.
- The tuxedo jacket, launched for women by Yves Saint Laurent, set the stage for the future of womenswear-that-is-menswear. In one simple statement, the adoption of *Le Smoking* jacket in fashion allowed for a future where women didn't have to wear pretty dresses to feel feminine.

■ **LEFT:** Bell-bottom pants revivals have occurred numerous times across the history of fashion, but were particularly prevalent in the Sixties.